CONVERSATIONAL CB
The Language of the Hiway

MW00915503

by **DAVID ECKSTEIN GOLDMAN**

IMPORTANT NOTE

It must be noted that the Citizen's Band is regulated by the Federal Communications Commission (FCC) and all CB operators are required to be licensed and required to familiarize themselves with its proper rules and regulations. Wherever there are conflicts or inconsistencies between what is found herein and the FCC rules and regulations, the FCC rules and regulations take precedence. Wherever there are conflicts or inconsistencies between the contents herein and state and local traffic laws, the latter should be observed.

ISBN: 1-4782-4079-2
ISBN-13: 9781478240792

PREFACE

This is a primer for the newcomer to the wonderful world of CB hiway driving. When the author once asked, "How do you talk on the CB radio?" he received the answer, "You don't quote Shakespeare." It's true. The author then set out to learn what one does say on the radio. When living in France, you speak French. When living in Spain, you speak Spanish. When talking on a Citizen's Band Radio, you speak CB. This then is a primer on conversational CB. It is a primer of dialogue that is drawn from the world of hiway driving. Please note that it is meant as a manual for the instruction of a new language and is NOT a manual for (1) the obstruction of justice in the enforcement of traffic laws, or (2) the circumvention of FCC rules and regulations. The author of this primer is himself a licensed CB operator who has enjoyed the world of CB. Much of his hiway driving has been on that stretch of hiway from Springfield, Illinois to St. Louis, Missouri. For that reason he has chosen to use hiway I55 in his examples herein. Enjoy this manual. 3's and 8's to you.

CONVERSATIONAL CB
The Language of the Hiway

YOU'RE ON THE ROAD

Well, you just got your radio and now you're going for a drive. You just turned it on and you hear all kinds of noise. Please note that it will be several days before your ears will become attuned to the radio. At first you'll feel like you're in a taxicab and you won't be able to make heads or tails out of all the noise. After a couple of days' listening you'll be able to actually discover words in the sound coming out of your radio, but you probably won't know what they mean. That is because they are part of a new language: conversational CB.

You now turn onto the hiway. All you hear is static and a few distant voices. Why? Because you haven't tuned to channel 19 (pronounced *"one-nine"*). While not officially recognized as such by the FCC, channel 19 is the hiway channel. By turning to channel 19 you have become a member of the world's most exciting fraternity: mobile hiway CBers.

The first thing you must do is to familiarize yourself with the direction of the road on which you are driving. You must know if you are heading north, south, east or west. Why? Because if you are heading south and you want to know what the road conditions ahead of you are like you will want to converse with *("shout to")* a northbound CBer. Why do you want a northbound CBer if you are headed south? You want a northbound CBer because he has already traveled on that stretch of hiway *("black and white sea," "boulevard")* toward which you are heading.

The second thing you must do is to familiarize yourself with the mile markers on the hiway. They are the little sign markers sticking up near the shoulder of the hiway with little numbers on them. For example, if you are driving south on I55 *("double nickle")* from Springfield, Illinois to St. Louis, Missouri the mile markers will go from higher numbers to smaller numbers as you move south. As you travel north from St. Louis *("the Gateway City")* to Springfield *("the Capital City")* and on to Chicago *("the Windy City")* the numbers go from smaller to higher. As you move south from Springfield to St. Louis the numbers tell you how many miles you are from St. Louis. The same is true as you move north from St. Louis to Springfield: the mile markers tell you how far you are out of St. Louis. This, of course, will vary from hiway to hiway, but once you become familiar with the hiway on which you are traveling the mile markers will allow you to discern whether or not a fellow CBer with whom you are talking is in front of you or behind you.

Now that you are on the hiway the radio is important to you for many reasons, some of which are:

1) It allows you to find out what road conditions are like ahead of you;

2) It allows you to know what weather conditions are like ahead of you;

3) It allows you to get directions to find gas stations *("find go-juice")*, restaurants *("put the feedbag on")*, restrooms *("10-100")*, and where to stop for coffee *("take a coffee break")*;

4) It allows you to report accidents on the road and any irregular driving habits of those around you;

5) And more . . .

Back to the road. You are traveling down the hiway and you hear a voice say, "Break 19" (pronounced *"one-nine"*). That means "I want to talk on the channel and I'm looking for someone to answer me." If nobody else is currently talking, you respond, "Go breaker," meaning go ahead and talk (or you say *"go," "come on breaker," "come ahead,"* or *"come ahay"*). If others are already talking they should say "In just a minute *('in a short', 'in a short-short')* breaker we will be done and you can go ahead and talk." If the talkers are a distance away and are not coming through real loud and clear on the radio, you can probably say "come ahay" to the "breaker" anyway without being rude to other talkers. Manners are important, so always ask for a "break," especially when you are off the hiway and in a town area.

When you are on the hiway you can combine your "break" with some qualifications so as to not only get a "come ahead breaker" but also to get the person you want. An example of this is "Break 19 for a northbound 155." The CBer who answers you *("gives you a comeback")* will be a northbound CBer who will say, "You've got a northbound 55, come on." Now it's your turn to respond to his "come back." You want to know what the road ahead of you is like, so you say, "How's she looking back over your shoulder, old buddy?" His reply will tell you. If you want to know what weather conditions lie ahead of you, then you ask, "How's the weather looking back over your shoulder, old buddy?" If you just ask, "How's she looking back over your shoulder," chances are you will get a report *("come back")* on speed traps *("10-73," "smokey report")*. Once you get your answer *("come back")*, manners demand that you tell your "old buddy" what the road is like behind you *("how things are looking back over your shoulder")*. You may wonder why you are calling a total stranger "old buddy." That's simple. All CBers belong to a close-knit fraternity. Whether a CBer drives a large truck *("18 wheeler," "big rig")* or a small car *("4 wheeler")* he is there to help his fellow CBers and all other citizens. As the saying goes, "We're all in this together," so we all work together and help each other as friends.

During your conversation "old buddy" will probably ask, "Who we got there?" That means "To whom am I speaking?" He wants to know your name, but not your actual name. He wants to know your "handle," that is, your CB nickname. When you get your CB license, the FCC gives you your legal name, or in other words, the FCC gives you a set of call numbers: 3 letters and 4 numbers. But CBers also use nicknames *("handles")* in conjunction with their call letters, and once they have come on the air and announced their call letters they will normally just use their nicknames ("handles") until they sign off. So whatever nickname you feel is appropriate, you assume that name as your "handle." Whether or not it conforms to FCC rules and regulations, most hiway travelers use only their handle and not their call letters while on the road. So you answer back, "You got that _____ [your handle], who we got there?" He will respond by telling you his "handle," after which you will know the CB name ("handle") of a new friend.

BASIC NUMBERS

						1
2	3	4	5	6	7	8
9	10	11	12	13	14	15
16	17	18	19	20	21	22
23/30	24	25	26	27	28	29

I don't want to confuse you, but now let's throw in some basic numbers that will help you to converse while you travel along the hiway. You will hear *"10-4," "10-20," "10-36," "10-100," "3's"* *and "8's"* and more. In order to simplify communications, CBers utilize what is known as the 10-Code. It is a short hand numerical way of asking questions, giving answers, and reporting accidents and problems while on the road. On page 19 of this manual you will find a copy of the 10-Code, but at this point I wish to familiarize you with the most commonly used numbers. To say "yes" or "I understand" or "I agree" you say *"10-4."* Many CBers embellish on this and say *"Roger 4-10"* or *"4-10"* or *"Roger-D"* or *"Roger D-4."* All of these are regularly used and each is interchangeable for the other. When a CBer answers you on the road *("gives you a comeback")* and you want to know his location on the hiway, you ask him, "What is your 10-20?" or simply, "What's your 20?" He'll then look to see what mile marker he is near and will then relay that to you along with what direction he is headed. Many times you will hear someone ask for a *"10-36."* That means "What time is it?" Your answer is "10-36 is _____ [time]." If anyone ever asks you for a "10-36," be nice and give him the correct time. There will be times you will hear "$300 radio and no watch." When you hear that it is just good-natured kidding on the radio. If you are stopping to visit a restroom you are *"going*

10-100." The numerical expression *"3's to you"* means "best regards" and *"8's to you"* means "love and kisses." By saying *"Good numbers on you"* or *"We send you good numbers"* you are covering all bases without sounding "fresh" to another CBer. You are probably wondering when you use "3's" and "8's" anyway. Well, you use them after you've conversed with someone and you're closing the conversation. When closing a conversation you may also add, *"Well, we better back on out of here."* That means "Well, we better be going." You can throw in "good numbers" with that.

We've covered a lot of ground so far, so let me put it together as far as we've gotten into an example dialogue:

CB #1: Break 19 for a northbound I55.

CB #2: You got one, come on.

CB #1: Who we got there?

CB #2: You got that Deerhunter.

CB #1: 10-4 Deerhunter, how we looking over your shoulder?

CB #2: You're clean to that 62 mile marker, that's where we got on the old boulevard. Who we got there?

CB #1: You got that Yo-Yo.

CB #2: What's your 20 there Yo-Yo?

CB #1: We're at the 79.

CB #2: 10-4 Yo-Yo, we're at the 76. How we looking back over your shoulder northbound?

CB #1: You got a clean shot into that Capital City.

CB #2: 10-4. We thank you for that comeback. Well, we better back on out of here. 3's to you Yo-Yo. You got that Deerhunter northbound and down. We gone, by-by.

CB #1: Roger-D. 3's to you for the comeback. Yo-Yo doing it southbound. By-by.

SMOKEY REPORTS

Now what would have happened if either one had something to report? Well, we will discuss that now. When traveling down the hiway CBers report to each other the location of police vehicles (whether it is legally proper or not), road conditions, weather conditions, accidents, and other points of interest. If someone asks you for a *"smokey report,"* they want to know the location of any police vehicles on the road, if there are any. That which follows will tell you how to respond. A *"bear"* is a policeman or police car. A police car with markings, red lights *("gumballs," "cherries")* and possibly radar, is referred to as a *"tijuana taxi."* An unmarked police car is a *"plain wrapper"* and if it's blue it's a *"plain blue wrapper,"* if it's green it's a *"plain green wrapper"* and so on. A local city police car is a *"local yokel"* and a sheriff or deputy police car is a *"county mounty."* A police plane or helicopter *("chopper")* is a *"bear in the air," "spy in the sky,"* or *"eye in the sky."* A police car sitting in the median is a *"bear in the median"* or a *"bear in the grass."* If the police car has a radar machine it is a *"picture taker"* or a *"smokey shining a laser beam."* When reporting a "picture taker" it is important to notice if the radar is pointing toward the north, south, east or west bound lanes of traffic. If it is pointing north, then you report that the "picture taker is working the north bound side." If you can't tell, then you merely report the "picture taker" and his location ("20"). If the police car is moving in traffic you report a *"smokey on the move"* and you give his location and the direction he is traveling. When you get a report of a police car in the median or on the side of the road, when you drive by that spot it is your responsibility to report whether or not he is still there as you go by. If he's still there, you report that you see him by saying, "I just put an eyeball on the smokey at the _____ [mile marker], he's still there." If he is gone when you get there, you report that "it's all clean at the _____ [mile marker]" and that "the smokey must have flopped back on the road heading [give the direction if you know it]." When a policeman stops someone for speeding and gives him a ticket, that's referred to as *"handing out green stamps."* The car that was stopped is *"feeding the bears"* and all CBers know that they *"don't want any green stamps for their album."* If you are driving down the hiway and a car without a CB radio *("doesn't have a set of ears")* passes you on the left moving in excess of the speed limit *("with the hammer down"),* he is referred to as *"bear bait."* Why? He doesn't know where the police are, and thus if there are any on the road in front of him he will flush them out and get stopped for speeding.

When a policeman pulls a car over onto the shoulder to write out a speeding ticket or for any other reason, that's referred to as *"having a bear with a 4-wheeler on the side"* and chances are the police car will have its lights flashing *("the gumballs going").* Many times as you are traveling down the hiway you will see a car, camper, or trailer off on the side of the road or in the median. It is important to find out whether or not it is a disguised police vehicle. When you go by it you should look to see if it has radar equipment. If it is not a police vehicle then it is *"clean."* You should report the vehicle, its location ("20") and whether or not it is "clean." Always check overpasses and exit ramps from the overpasses onto the hiway for a "picture taker" with his "laser beam" aimed down onto your side or the other side of the hiway.

Now let me give you a sample dialogue of the above material so you will understand "smokey reports":

CB #1:   How about a southbound 155.

CB #2:   You got one, come on.

CB #1:   This is the Roadrunner, who we got?

CB #2:   You got that Ditchdigger, Roadrunner, come on.

CB #1:   10-4. How we looking back over your shoulder?

CB #2:   You're clean to that 53 where you've got a picture taker. He's working that northbound side so back off the hammer at the 53. You've also got a tijuana taxi northbound and on the move at the 56. How we looking back over your shoulder?

CB #1:   Roger-D. You got a bear in the air over the 43. You got a bear with a four-wheeler on the side handing out green stamps at the 41.

CB #2:   10-4 Roadrunner. How about that exit ramp at that junction 140. We heard a report of a picture taker there a short [a little while] ago.

CB #1:   Negator there, Ditchdigger. That exit ramp was clean when we passed by. We didn't put an eyeball on any picture taker.

CB #2:   10-4 old buddy. We sure thank you for that info. Mercy sakes for sure. Well, 3's to you. Ditchdigger southbound and down.

CB #1:   Thanks for that comeback Ditchdigger. Good numbers on you. Roadrunner northbound and down. By-by.

HIWAY POSITION

When traveling on the hiway it is also very important to know your position on the road in relation to other CBers traveling in the same direction as you. If you are traveling southbound and you hear a call ("shout") from another southbound CBer, ask him his location ("20"). If he is in front of you he has the *"front door"* or *"lead"* position. In that instance, since you are behind him, you have the *"back door"* position. If there is a CBer in front of you ("front door") and one behind you ("back door"), you have the middle position, called the *"rocking chair"* position. The "front door" or "lead" truck or car has the responsibility of keeping you informed as to all police vehicles or important road conditions in front of you in the southbound lane (if you're all heading southbound) and moving toward you in the northbound lane. The "back door" CBer has the responsibility of keeping you and your "front door" informed of all police vehicles that come in behind you from exit ramps or any other place. The "back door" CBer by watching everything behind you is *"shaking up the bushes"* for you and your "front door." It is your responsibility as the "rocking chair" to report any police vehicles that happen to get in between you and the "front door" and to relay all messages from your "front door" to your "back door" and vice versa. If you are all close enough that the "front door" can receive radio transmissions from your "back door" then you don't have to relay each of their transmissions since they can each *"get a copy"* on the other. If you are the "front door" you must always report any police vehicles that are heading toward you in the opposite, on-coming lanes of traffic. Why? Because sometimes the police vehicle will travel northbound for several miles and then turn onto an exit ramp, cross over on the overpass and enter back onto the southbound lanes of the hiway. That is referred to as a *"flip-flop."* Some police cars will work a 10 or 20 mile stretch of the hiway on both sides by "flip-flopping" all day. As you are conversing with your "front door" and "back door," if you have trouble understanding something that is said and you want it repeated you say, *"how about a comeback on that."* If you have trouble hearing something that is said over the radio you say, *"how about a comeback on that, I couldn't get a copy."* Or you can use the 10-Code short hand form and ask for a repeat of the transmission by use of the numbers *"10-9"*; you say, *"how about a 10-9 on that."* If you ask a question and the answer is "no" instead of "yes" ("10-4"), the other CBer will answer your questions with *"negator,"* *"negative,"* or *"negatory."* If other CBers on the hiway talk while you are talking their voices may block yours out. In that case your transmission has been *"walked on."* The CBer for whom the transmission was meant will ask you to repeat your transmission. Below is a sample dialogue of the above:

CB #1: Break for a southbound I55.

CB #2: You got that Crapshooter, come on.

CB #1: 10-4 Crapshooter, how we looking over your shoulder northbound?

CB #2: You got a clean shot into that Capital City. Haven't seen a thing since we came out of there.

CB #1: 10-4 old buddy. You're clean to that Litchfield town where we got on.

CB #3: Break for that northbounder.

CB #1: You got that northbounder.

CB #3: 10-4. Who we got there and what's your 20?

CB #1: You got that Mickey-mouse and we're doing it northbound past that 49 mile marker.

CB #3: Roger-D Mickey-mouse. You got that Breadmaker. Looks like you got that front door. We're northbound at the 45. We'll shake up the bushes at your back door if you'll run the front.

CB #1:	Ay-Roger-D old Breadmaker.
CB #3:	Mickey-mouse I heard a report earlier of a northbound smokey on the move at the 55.
CB #1:	Negator on the mobile smokey. I just had a comeback from a southbounder out of that Capital City and he said he hadn't put an eyeball on anything.
CB #3:	That smokey must have done a flip-flop so we'll keep our eyes open for him mobiling south.
CB #1:	Breadmaker, you want to comeback on that. You got walked on and I couldn't get a copy.
CB #3:	10-4 Mickey-mouse, I said that smokey must have done a flip-flop. We'll keep our eyes open and let you know if we see him mobiling south.
CB #1:	That's a big 10-4.

REPORTING OTHER MATTERS

Hiway traveling also demands that you be alert to other matters in addition to making "smokey reports." As a licensed CB operator you have a duty to report accidents when and if you see them. An accident is reported in several steps. First you announce an emergency on the road by saying *"Break 19 for an emergency."* Then, in order to report a vehicular accident you report a *"10-33"* and give the location of the accident by reporting its "20." The second step is to try to locate a policeman on the channel by asking, *"Is there a smokey on channel 19; break for a state smokey, there's been an accident."* If a policeman is in the vicinity and monitoring channel 19 *("on channel")* he will hear your "break" and respond. If you get no answer, known as a *"negative contact,"* then you should ask for a "break" to try to reach a CB operated by someone in his home *("base station")* near the hiway. To make contact with a "base station" you say *"Break 19 for an emergency. How about a base station out there, I've got a 10-33 to report."* If you get an answer ("comeback") from a "base station" then give them all of the information and they will contact

"You've got a base station . . ."

the proper authorities by telephone. A telephone call is a *"land line."* If you are unable to reach either a policeman on the hiway or a "base station," then you should move your radio dial from channel 19 to channel 9 and report the accident and listen for a response. Why? Channel 9 is the national emergency channel that is monitored 24 hours a day for any and all emergency calls. There may be times however when you get no response on channel 9 because you are too far away from any channel 9 monitors for them to receive your transmission *("signal")*. If that happens, move to other channels on your radio and try to locate a "base station." If after that you have had no success in locating help, return to channel 19 and keep reporting the accident to other drivers so they can join you in an effort to locate proper help. It is also important to notify other drivers of the accident so that they will drive carefully by the location of the accident and thus avoid any further mishaps.

Example dialogue:

CB #1: Break 19 for an emergency.

CB #2: Go Breaker.

CB #1: There's a 10-33 at the 77 mile marker. Are there any smokies on channel listening? How about a base station out there. We've got an emergency here on I55.

CB #2: Must not be any smokies or bases on channel, old buddy. You drop down to channel 9 and I'll keep shouting here on 19 for some help.

CB #1: 10-4. We thank you. [move to channel 9] We got an emergency situation on I55. How about somebody monitoring channel 9, you got a copy? [no response — move to other channels and "break" for base stations] Break 15 for a base station. We got a 10-33 to report.

CB #3: Come ahead on that 10-33.

CB #1: 10-4. You got an accident at the 77 mile marker on the southbound side of I55.

CB #3: Roger-D. We'll take care of it. We'll landline the state police.

Aside from accidents, you should also be alert to and report improper and unsafe driving habits of others on the road. If a car is tailgating other cars you should warn other CBers to be careful of that driver. You should also report other drivers who are driving down the center of the hiway, taking up part of each lane. It is important to report extremely slow moving vehicles so other CBers don't come upon the slow vehicles too fast to pass. Vehicles on the shoulder should be reported so that approaching CBers are careful not to side-swipe the vehicle. If you should ever notice a car weaving down the road, it is possible that the driver of the vehicle is driving while intoxicated *("dwi")*. You should definitely report that to other CBers and also to any "smokies" on the channel to prevent a serious accident. You will undoubtedly hear a report of *"pretty seat covers"* while you are traveling down the hiway. "Pretty seat covers" means there is an attractive young lady in the vehicle. Example dialogue:

"But sir, I didn't mean your girl-friend when I said I wanted to strip your seat covers."

CB #1: Break 19.

CB #2: Go.

CB #1: 10-4. You southbounders be careful of the 4-wheeler on the shoulder at the 49. His tail is still partly on the hiway.

CB #3: 10-4. We thank you for that report.

CB #4: How about that southbounder past the 49.

CB #1: You got him.

CB #4: Yeah old buddy. You'll be putting your eyeball on some pretty seat covers in a short. They're in a little green 4-wheeler with Illinois tags [license plates]. We just passed them a short ago.

CB #1: Maybe if I ask her nicely she'll join me.

CB #4: Negator. She's with her better-half [boyfriend or husband].

RADIO CHECK

"Break for a radio check."

You should also be familiar with the *"radio check."* Many times when you are on the radio ("on channel") you will hear "Break for a radio check." What is a "radio check"? It is someone asking you how strongly his signal is being transmitted or *"how he's getting out."* He wants to know if he sounds clear, if his modulation is good, and how far away you are from him so he can judge his transmitting distance capability. If your CB radio has a meter on it, then you can tell the CBer asking for the radio check what kind of a meter reading you are getting from him when he transmits to you. The needle on your meter will point to a number. It is that number that you relate ("shout") to him to let him know how he is *"coming in,"* *"coming in on your meter,"* *"hitting your meter,"* or *"hitting you."* If his signal is extremely strong then he is *"throwing a bodacious signal."* If he is a great distance away and he is transmitting an extremely strong signal, it is possible he has a power amplifier called a *"linear"* connected to his radio. Operating your radio is referred to as *"running the radio."* If a CBer uses a "linear" that is referred to as *"running a linear."* If he is transmitting without a "linear" he is *"running barefoot."* To find out how far away the other CBer is you simply ask him for his location or "what's your 20." If the sound of the transmission is too loud with a lot of background noise you tell him that his *"modulation is too high."* Many CBers use what is known as a *"power mike."* A "power mike" is a microphone that has a dial that allows its user to raise or lower his voice amplification or "modulation." If the "modulation is too high," meaning too loud, you tell the CBer to turn it down. If the voice is too faint, you tell him to "turn up your power mike" if he is using one. If you are getting a good transmission from him but he is not receiving your return transmission very well or vice versa, you might advise him to check the standing wave ratio between his antenna and his radio *("SWR's")*. If his transmission to you is choppy or *"is breaking up"* he might have a short in his microphone. Example dialogue:

CB #1:   Break for a radio check.
CB #2:   Come ahead radio check, we got you.
CB #1:   D-4. How we coming in over there?
CB #2:   Give me a three count and I'll give you a meter reading.
CB #1:   1-2-3.
CB #2:   You're throwing us a 10 pounder. You got one bodacious signal.
CB #1:   10-4. How's our modulation?
CB #2:   Very good. We got you wall to wall tree top tall. Are you running a linear?
CB #1:   Negator. We're running barefoot.
CB #2:   10-4.
CB #1:   Thanks for the radio check.

There may be times when you are listening to your radio that you will hear very strange noises that sound as if they are from a science fiction movie soundtrack. They may be followed by "breakers" asking for someone *"out in skipland."* *"Skip"* is the transmission of CB radio signals over great distances due to atmospheric conditions that allow them to "skip" farther than normal transmissions travel. It is possible to talk to other CBers over 600 miles away when "skipland comes in."

SIGNING OFF

Important to your proficiency in conversational CB is an understanding of the proper techniques for ending a transmission, known as *"signing off."* The ending of transmission, or "signing off" can take 3 forms:

1) Merely ending your immediate discussion but keeping your radio turned on and listening until you wish to speak again;

2) Ending your communication with a CBer headed in the opposite direction since his signal will become too weak for you to receive as you both travel in your own different directions, and since you've both already reported to each other the information requested; you still have your radio turned on;

3) Ending communication with those to whom you have been conversing and then turning off your radio.

When you merely end your immediate conversation but still have your radio turned on ("still on channel") and you are listening to what others say, you are doing what is known as *"staying on the side listening."* In 10-Code short hand you are *"being 10-8"* or *"being 10-10."* Normally, when traveling on the hiway, if you are traveling with someone as your "front door" or "back door" you will report to him anything you see and hear and in between such reports to him you merely listen to the radio *"standing by"* to hear anything new from him or from other CBers. In that way you avoid crowding the channel with unnecessary chatter. Those who talk incessantly on the radio are referred to as *"ratchet jaws"* or *"bucket mouths."* When you end transmission to a CBer driving *("trucking," "pedaling,"* or *"doing it")* in the opposite direction, you thank him for any information he gave you. Most CBers send "good numbers" to each other in this instance and many will "sign off" to a vehicle *("rig")* headed in the opposite direction with a little poetry. Below are some of the "signing off" poems you may hear on the hiway:

> *Truck 'em easy, truck 'em light*
> *Have a good today, and a better tonight.*
> *[Handle] northbound and down.*
> *We gone. By-by.*

> *If you're going to pedal it over 55*
> *You pedal 'em easy and arrive alive.*
> *[Handle], we doing it southbound.*

> *Keep the big one between the ditches*
> *The little one in your britches.*
> *[Handle] . . .*

> *Truck 'em easy, truck 'em neat*
> *Keep all 18 wheels upon the street.*
> *[Handle] . . .*

If you want all your dreams to be real
Stay awake behind the wheel.
[Handle] . . .

"This is the Big Trucker.
We'll be 10-7 at the Truck-
em-up stop."

When you end transmission completely and turn off your radio you are "signing off" completely. In 10-Code it is known as *"going 10-7"* or *"being 10-7."* It is also referred to as *"pulling the big switch"* or *"cutting the old coax."* The "coax" is the connecting cable between your antenna and your radio.

BACK IN TOWN

When you leave the hiway and are driving into town, it is advisable to switch to a channel other than 19. Channel 11 is the *"national call channel."* That means that if you want to make radio contact with another CBer you ask for him on channel 11. That is known as giving him a *"call," "shout"* or *"holler."* Once you reach the CBer you're "calling for" *("make contact")* you both should switch to another channel to converse. Going to another channel is referred to in 10-Code as *"10-27 to channel _____ ."* If you ask for a "break" on channel 11 and "call" for another CBer and he doesn't respond, then you say *"thank you for the break, negative contact on that _____ [handle]."* The 10-Code equivalent of "negative contact" is *"10-77"* or you can say *"double 7's."* Remember, once you are off the hiway, always ask for a "break" before talking to someone. And never use channel 9 for idle talk *("chitchat")* because it is the "national emergency channel." Example dialogue:

CB #1:   Break 11. [pronounced *one-one*]

CB #2:   Go "Break 11."

CB #1:   Thank you for that go. How about that Deputy Dog. How about you Deputy Dog, we looking. [no response from Deputy Dog] Double 7's on that Deputy Dog. Cheyenne Kid. We be clear and on the side.

CB #3:   Break 11.

CB #2:   Go.

CB #3:   We thank you for that go. How about you Cheyenne Kid. Deputy Dog looking for that Cheyenne Kid.

CB #1:   You got that Cheyenne Kid, Deputy Dog, let's 10-27 to that 15 [pronounced *one-five*].

CB #3:   10-4.

RADIO ETIQUETTE

"My mother taught me not to throw carriers, so I said, 'Quit keying your mike, you cotton-picker.'"

It is important to avoid the use of abusive language over the radio. The use of foul language is prohibited by FCC regulations. In 10-Code it is referred to as a "10-30", meaning it does not conform to FCC regulations. The harshest word that one should use on the radio is the noun "cotton-picker" and the adjective "cotton-picking." They are used as substitutes for foul words by CBers. By all means, when you are on the radio and you find the need to use foul language, please limit yourself to either the noun "cotton-picker" or the adjective "cotton-picking."

Example dialogue:

CB #1: Break for a southbound I55.
CB #2: You got a southbounder, come on.
CB #1: Be careful of that cotton-picking tire in the center of this old boulevard at the 41.
CB #2: 10-4 old buddy. We thank you. We'll keep our eyes open for that cotton-picker.

Remember, whether you're a big truck ("18 wheeler") or a small car ("4 wheeler") when you turn to channel 19 on the hiway you are a member of the world's most exciting fraternity — the fraternity of mobile CBers. Being a member of that fraternity, you have a responsibility to use the radio properly. Never give false reports or put the microphone up to your car radio to play music. Avoid activating your microphone *("keying the mike")* unless you have something to say. By "keying the mike" you are blocking the transmission of someone else who might be trying to transmit within your radio's range. If you say nothing after "keying the mike," you are merely jamming the channel which is known as *"throwing carriers."* That can be very distracting, and can interfere with important transmissions.

Below are a short story and a poem written by the author in conversational CB. Use the primer and its glossary to help you understand.

A SHORT STORY IN CONVERSATIONAL CB

It was a bright, sunny morning in the Gateway City when I climbed into my rig to truck on through that Capital City town of Illinois on my way to that Barley-pop Capital via the Windy City. I was hopping onto that double nickle when I heard somebody shout, "How about that Old King Cole?"

"10-4," I said. "You got him, come on back."

"10-4 old buddy, you got that Jolly Roger, what's your 20?"

"I'm at the 17," I answered.

"Yeah good buddy, mercy sakes, I got a good copy on you. I'm at that 13, looks like you got that front, I'll shake up the bushes here at your back."

"10-4 Jolly Roger." Well, we were pedaling up that old boulevard together northbound when a 4-wheeler went flying by us on the side with his hammer down . . . "Didn't see any ears on that 4-wheeler Jolly, did you?"

"Negator there Old Kinger. He had his better-half with him and he's flying like bear bait."

"That's a big 10-4 on his better-half. Mighty fine seat covers all right." Sure enough, two miles up the road that old 4-wheeler was off on the side taking some green stamps from a tijuana taxi. "Be careful there Jolly, you got some gumballs going there at the 22. That old bear will be hopping back on this black and white sea in a short mobiling north."

"10-4 Kinger. If he hops in between us I hope he enjoys that old rocking chair."

There weren't many northbounders with ears as we were pedaling north, but I heard a lot of southbound breakers asking for smokey reports. I told them to legal needle through that Litchfield-town area because she was wall to wall bears. Even saw a spy in the sky over the 33. As I was pedaling in near the Capital City by the bears' den, I heard some base with a comeback that was enough to blow my windows out. "Wall to wall tree top tall," was all I could tell him when he asked for a radio check. I asked him if he was running a linear and he said, "Negator, we've just got a bodacious signal."

As Jolly Roger and I rounded Springfield town we picked up another rig mobiling north to that Bloomington-town. He didn't stop talking for one minute. He jumped off at that Bloomington-town shouting, "3's to you Old King Cole. We thank you for that front door. You truck 'em easy, you truck 'em light, have a good today and a better tonight. We hope to catch you on the flipper if we don't flop her. We better back on out of here. We gone by-by." With that, Jolly Roger said, "Real ratchet jaw."

"10-4 to that. In order to give your ears a rest, old buddy, we'll be 10-10 and 10-8 on the side till we see something," I said. A mile later I heard, "Break 19." It was somebody breaking for a weather report, so I told him he was clean to the chicken coups about the 10, where some of that white stuff was still sitting on the road. Jolly Roger and I stopped for a coffee break at the truck-em-up stop outside of the Windy. He said, "Hey old buddy, when we get into that Barley-pop Capital let's take in some loose juice."

"For shay," I said. We did.

A CB VERSE

11 p.m. and we're back on the road
Pedaling to the Windy with a barley-pop load.
Break one-nine came over the set,
Come on breaker, who did I get?
You got that Bigrigger, break one-nine,
You got that Ditchdigger, you're coming in fine.
How do we look back over your shoulder?
You're clean to the six-three, but the weather is colder.
Ay 10-4 and thanks, we southbound and down.
For the next 10 miles we heard not a sound.
I wasn't worried and had not a care
Cause I didn't see a single old bear.
Break one-nine for a radio check,
Please wait breaker, we're reporting a wreck.
A 10-33 down by the ramps,
I thought it was someone getting green stamps.
I hope everyone's fine, was my immediate call,
Roger-D-4, but there's bears wall to wall.
As we pedaled on into that Old Windy City
We saw some seat covers and reported them pretty.
Well, we're down and we're home and it feels just like heaven,
So old Ditchdigger trucker is going 10-7.

Well, that ends the text of the first primer on Conversational CB. I hope you have enjoyed it and that it has proved a worthwhile, educational manual for you. Listed below is a glossary of common conversational CB terminology. Following that you will find a copy of the 10-Code. Enjoy your radio. Respect others. Welcome to the world of CB.

GLOSSARY

AM	CB frequencies
Back	Over to you
Back door	Rear vehicle
Back down	Drive more slowly
Back on out	End transmission and just listen
Band aid wrapper	Ambulance
Barefoot	Transmit without any power amplification
Barley-pop	Beer
Base station	Home or business operated CB
Beam	Directional antenna
Bear	Policeman or police car
Bear bait	Speeding car without a CB
Bears' den	Police headquarters
Bear in the air	Police airplane
Bear in the grass	Police vehicle in the median
Bear with ears	Police vehicle with a CB
Beaver	Female
Better-half	Boyfriend, girlfriend, husband, wife
Big rig	Truck and trailer
Big 10-4	An emphatic Yes
Black and white sea	Hiway
Black gold	Oil
Black top	Hiway
Bleed over	Transmission from one channel interfering with transmission on another channel
Bodacious	Strong signal
Bodacious	Outspoken person (adjective)
Boulevard	Hiway
Break	Let me talk
Breaker	One who asks to talk
Bucket mouth	Incessant talker
Carrier	Activate the microphone without talking
Catch	Talk to
CB	Citizens' Band Radio
CBer	One who uses a CB Radio
Channel jockey	One who uses a CB Radio
Chickadee	Female
Chicken coop	Truck weigh station
Chopper	Police helicopter

Clean	Not a police vehicle; no police in sight
Clear	Ending transmission
Coax	Cable connecting radio and antenna
Coffee break	Meeting other CBers for coffee
Coin gate	Toll bridge
Come again	Please repeat
Come ahead	You may talk
Comeback	Responding message
Convoy	Several trucks in a row
Copy	Receive the transmission
Cotton-picker	Foul descriptive noun
Cotton-picking	Foul descriptive adjective
County mounty	Sheriff vehicle
Covered up	Interfered with
Cut the coax	Turn off the radio
D-4	Yes
Double "L"	Telephone call
Double "7's"	Negative contact with another CBer
DWI	Driving while intoxicated
Ears	CB Radio
Ears on	Having your radio turned on
Eighteen wheeler	Big truck
Eights	Love and kisses
Eighty-eights	Love and kisses
Eyeball	To see something
Feed the bears	Receive a speeding ticket
Final	Last transmission
Flake	Goofy person
Flakey	Goofy
Flip flop	Turn around and go in the opposite direction
Four wheeler	Car
Friendly candy company	FCC
Front door	Lead vehicle
Getting out	Transmission being heard
Go juice	Gasoline
Gone	Final transmission or switching to another channel
Good buddy	Fellow CBer
Green stamps	Speeding ticket
Hammer	Gas pedal
Hammer down	Speeding
Handing out green stamps	Writing a speeding ticket
Handle	CBer's CB nickname

Handy-talky	Walkie talkie
Hard black gold	Coal
Hard black stuff	Coal
High gear	Use of power amplifier to increase transmission power
Holler	Call to another CBer
Home 20	Location of one's home
How about	Calling to . . .
Key the mike	Activate the microphone
Landline	Telephone call
Laser beam	Police radar
Laser gun	Police radar gun
Lead	Vehicle in front of another
Legal needle	Driving 55 MPH
Linear	Power amplifier to increase transmission output
Local yokel	City police
Loose juice	Alcoholic beverage
Mail	Conversations that are overheard
Mercy sakes	Gee whiz
Mile marker	Small sign along hiway with mile numbers on it
Mobile	CB in a moving vehicle
Mobile	On the move
Modulate	To talk on a CB
Negative	No
Negative contact	No response from party being called
Negative copy	Not being able to hear the response transmitted
Negatory	No
Needle	Speedometer
One time	A quick contact
On the side	Standing by listening on the channel
On the side	On the shoulder of the hiway
Over your shoulder	The road behind you
Peanut butter in ears	Not listening to the CB or having it turned off
Pedal	To drive
Peepers	Headlights
Pick-em-up	Pick up truck
Picture taker	Police car with radar
Pit stop	Stop for gas or to use rest room
Plain wrapper	Unmarked police car
Pop a pill	Take a pill to stay awake

Pregnant roller skate	Volkswagen
Radidio	CB Radio
Radio check	Checking your radio's performance
Read	To hear
Rig	Truck
Rocking chair	To be between two other CBers
Roller skate	Small car
Roger	Yes
Rubber side	The tires of a truck or car
Seat covers	Pretty female
73's	Best regards
Shiny side	Top of truck; the cab of a truck
Short	Minute; second; short period of time
Shout	Call to
Skip	Atmospheric conditions allowing transmissions to be received and sent over great distances
Smokey	Policeman; police car
SWR's	Standing wave ratio
Tags	License plates
Taking pictures	Operating a radar machine
10-4	Yes
10-20	Location
10-36	Correct time
10-100	Go to the rest room
Ten roger	Yes
Tijuana taxi	Fully marked police car
Thermos bottle	Tanker truck
Thirds	Best regards
Threes	Best regards
Throw	To transmit
Trip	Strong signal
Twenty	Location
Uncle Freddy	FCC
Wacky tobacky	Marijuana
Walked on	To have your signal covered over by someone else thus blocking you out
Wall to wall tree top tall	To come in loud and clear
Wall to wall bears	Police all around
Wet stuff	Rain
White stuff	Snow
Wrapper	The outside of a vehicle

OFFICIAL NATIONAL CB 10-CODE

10-1	Receiving Poorly
10-2	Receiving Well
10-3	Stop Transmitting
10-4	OK, Message Received
10-5	Relay Message
10-6	Busy, Stand By
10-7	Out of Service, Leaving Air
10-8	In Service, Subject to Call
10-9	Repeat Message
10-10	Transmission Completed, Stand By
10-11	Talking Too Rapidly
10-12	Visitors Present
10-13	Advise Weather/Road Conditions
10-16	Make Pickup At _____
10-17	Urgent Business
10-18	Anything for Us?
10-19	Nothing for You, Return to Base
10-20	My Location is _____
10-21	Call by Telephone
10-22	Report in Person to _____
10-23	Stand by
10-24	Completed Last Assignment
10-25	Can You Contact _____?
10-26	Disregard Last Information
10-27	I Am Moving to Channel _____
10-28	Identify Your Station
10-29	Time is Up for Contact
10-30	Does Not Conform to FCC Rules
10-32	I Will Give You a Radio Check
10-33	EMERGENCY TRAFFIC AT THIS STATION
10-34	Trouble at this Station, Help Needed
10-35	Confidential Information
10-36	Correct Time is _____
10-37	Wrecker Needed at _____
10-38	Ambulance Needed at _____
10-39	Your Message Delivered
10-41	Please Tune to Channel _____
10-42	Traffic Accident at _____

10-43	Traffic Tieup at _____
10-44	I Have a Message for You (or) _____
10-50	Break Channel _____
10-60	What is Next Message Number?
10-62	Unable to Copy, Use Phone
10-63	Net Directed to _____
10-64	Net Clear
10-65	Awaiting Your Next Message/Assignment
10-67	All Units Comply
10-70	Fire at _____
10-71	Proceed with Transmission in Sequence
10-73	Speed Trap at _____
10-75	You Are Causing Interference
10-77	Negative Contact
10-81	Reserve Hotel Room for _____
10-82	Reserve Room for _____
10-84	My Telephone Number is _____
10-85	My Address is _____
10-89	Radio Repairman Needed at _____
10-90	I Have TVI
10-91	Talk Closer to Mike
10-92	Your Transmitter is Out of Adjustment
10-93	Check My Frequency on This Channel
10-94	Please Give Me a Long Count
10-95	Transmit Dead Carrier for 5 Seconds
10-99	Mission Completed, All Units Secure
10-100	Rest Stop
10-200	Police Needed at _____

Made in the USA
Las Vegas, NV
28 July 2023

75347207R00015